CODING CAREERS
IN **ENTERTAINMENT** AND **GAMES**

Cathleen Small

Cavendish
Square

New York

Published in 2020 by Cavendish Square Publishing, LLC
243 5th Avenue, Suite 136, New York, NY 10016

Copyright © 2020 by Cavendish Square Publishing, LLC

First Edition

Website: cavendishsq.com

Library of Congress Cataloging-in-Publication Data

Names: Small, Cathleen, author.
Title: Coding careers in entertainment and games / Cathleen Small.
Description: First edition. | New York : Cavendish Square, 2020. |
Series: Coding careers for tomorrow | Audience: Grades 7 to 12. |
Includes bibliographical references and index.
Identifiers: LCCN 2018055392 (print) | LCCN 2018056229 (ebook) |
ISBN 9781502645777 (ebook) | ISBN 9781502645760 (library bound) | ISBN 9781502645753 (pbk.)
Subjects: LCSH: Computer programming–Vocational guidance–
Juvenile literature. | Video games–Design–Juvenile literature. | Computer games–Design–
Juvenile literature. | Application software–Juvenile literature. | Vocational guidance.
Classification: LCC QA76.6115 (ebook) | LCC QA76.6115 .S63 2020 (print) |
DDC 005.1023–dc23
LC record available at https://lccn.loc.gov/2018055392

Editorial Director: David McNamara
Editor: Kristen Susienka
Copy Editor: Denise Larrabee
Associate Art Director: Alan Sliwinski
Designer: Ginny Kemmerer
Production Coordinator: Karol Szymczuk
Photo Research: J8 Media

Printed in the United States of America

Contents

The coding field is wide open to anyone with a knack for it and the necessary background or education for the job.

chapter_01

Introduction to Coding Careers

Back in the earliest days of video games, coding was incredibly simple. A very early video game, called *Tennis for Two*, was developed in 1958 by a physicist. In it, two lines appeared. One represented the net and the other the ground. A dot bounced from one side of the screen to the other, representing a tennis ball. People had controllers that allowed them to hit the ball back and forth. *Pong*, which was released by Atari in 1972 and is widely recognized as the earliest video game with mass appeal, wasn't much more complicated—it, too, involved a bouncing "ball" that was a graphical dot and a few lines designed to look like an overhead view of a Ping-Pong table. Everything was created in two dimensions, and one person could code a game in very little time.

Nowadays, video games are much more complicated, with realistic 3D graphics and worlds, highly interactive

Pong was the first arcade game to find mass-market appeal. It was simple but addictive!

game play, and often multiplayer functionality. While a single coder can still create a video game—and if the premise is interesting, it can be quite a fun game—mass-market games are developed by teams of coders working together, with each coder working on a specific piece of the game.

Gaming has crossed over into entertainment, as have the coding and technology. Blockbuster movies have been developed around games such as *Tomb Raider*, *Resident Evil*, and *Assassin's Creed*. The animation industry relies heavily on computer-generated animation and graphics techniques. Animation giant Pixar was founded by programmers and heavily funded by none other than Steve Jobs, the cofounder of Apple. Companies like Pixar have teams of programmers who create animation and automation tools that are used in the production of their animated films.

With the continued growth and development in both the gaming and entertainment fields, aspiring coders interested in the fields are sure to have ample career opportunities in the future.

WHAT IS CODING?

As a verb, the term "code" refers to writing programming lines that will create some sort of output. Examples of output include a website, a piece of software, or an application (app). When a person plays a video game or uses a website, that game or site exists because a coder or team of coders wrote the programming code that created it, including any graphics, features, and functionalities.

In a way, coders are like novelists. A novelist uses words to write a book, which is usually divided into chapters and sometimes parts. Regardless of how it's divided, the end product is a book. Similarly, a coder uses computer languages to write the code that will result in an end product, such as a website or an app. There are far too many programming languages to list them all, but some well-known ones are Python, HTML, and C++. Usually, a coder's end product is separated into parts too. Websites are made up of pages and sometimes frames on specific pages, as well as interactive versus static (nonmoving) elements. Apps are generally broken down into features and functions. For example, Venmo has the ability to send money to people, receive money from people, and transfer money from the app to your bank account. Social media has countless different features and functions, depending on the particular platform.

CODING IN GAMING

The career possibilities for coders are nearly endless, since almost every industry uses software or apps. Coders create

Good coders are needed in most every technology field. For avid gamers, a career in coding for games can be a perfect fit.

software for medical billing and some medical devices, software and applications for the military, financial software for those in the business and finance sector, and more. For aspiring coders who have a passion for gaming, the game industry is exploding and it is an excellent area in which to seek employment for a coding career.

There are many tech-related careers in gaming, including jobs in game design and story development. However, there is always a need for coders to actually write the games, once the game concepts have been designed and the

HISTORICAL FACES OF CODING: DANIELLE BUNTEN BERRY

Coding has historically been a heavily male-dominated field across the board, and that carries over to coding in the game and entertainment industries. Although a 2018 survey revealed that 45 percent of people who consider themselves gamers are female, according to a 2016 survey only 23 percent of game developers were female, and less than 2 percent were transgender. That makes Danielle Bunten Berry, a transgender American game designer and programmer, quite unique.

Berry began her career as a hobbyist game programmer in the 1970s and sold her first game to a software company in 1978. Over the following years, Berry sold numerous games to different software companies, including gaming giant Electronic Arts. After undergoing gender-reassignment surgery to transition from male to female in the early 1990s, Berry joked that she did so to bolster the number of females in the male-dominated field.

Berry died at the age of forty-nine from lung cancer, but her contributions to the field of gaming during her relatively short career were numerous. In 1998, soon before her death, the Computer Game Developers Association (now International Game Developers Association) bestowed on her the Lifetime Achievement Award, and in 2007 she was posthumously inducted into the Academy of Interactive Arts & Sciences Hall of Fame.

art created. For those who want to write the actual game code, the best programming language to learn depends on whether they're interested in systems programming or web programming.

Systems programming involves coding for stand-alone applications, such as video games that run strictly on gaming consoles. For this type of coding, the popular languages are C++, C#, and Java.

Director and animation supervisor Ramiro Lopez Dau works on a project at the Oculus Story Studio in San Francisco, California.

Web programming involves coding for applications that run on the internet. Popular languages for aspiring web coders are HTML5, CSS3, JavaScript, and SQL.

Most coders know multiple languages, though they often feel most comfortable in one—similar to how multilingual people are often most comfortable in their native language.

CODING IN ENTERTAINMENT

For those aspiring to code in the entertainment field, many of the common languages are similar to those used in game programming. C, C++, and C# are all commonly used in programming for animation. However, it can also be helpful to know the coding behind particular engines, such as Unreal, and frameworks, such as XNA.

It's important to note that working as an animator is *not* the same as coding. Animators work with prebuilt software to create animation sequences that ultimately are used in animations for film, television, or internet distribution. However, there are coders *behind* the animation software who may be hired by major animation companies, such as Pixar, to create proprietary animation tools, such as Pixar's RenderMan and Presto software packages. Programmers for games may program animations—after all, someone has to make that player graphic move throughout the game world!

Looking at the impact of coding on the gaming and entertainment industries is a good way to see how coders play an important role in both fields.

Before video games, there were pinball games—some with electronic components.

chapter_02

Coding's Impact on Entertainment and Gaming

The gaming and entertainment industries have existed for many generations, though they both look much different now that they incorporate technology. To understand the impact coding has had on these two industries, it helps to take a journey back through history and trace the changes in both.

A BRIEF HISTORY OF TECHNOLOGY

Currently, gaming and entertainment are multiplatform fields, which means games and entertainment can be enjoyed on everything from televisions to tablets to laptops to smartphones to gaming consoles. However, some of this technology has been developed relatively recently—much more recently than gaming and entertainment.

In the earliest days, entertainment generally took the form of oral storytelling, song, and dance, and gaming involved sporting events or a few strategy-based board games. Moving forward through history, plays became a common form of entertainment for the masses, followed by radio broadcasts and movies (first silent movies and then movies with sound).

By the middle of the twentieth century, though, televisions had become common in the United States, and television, films, and plays became the dominant forms of entertainment. Gaming existed in the form of board games and card games, as well as organized and semiorganized sports. Technology had reached entertainment but not gaming, which resulted in a big divide between the two fields. Entertainment was often driven by technology but was passive—people sat and watched television, a film, or a play—whereas gaming was interactive but virtually free of technological influence.

Eventually, the lines between gaming and entertainment blurred. More interactive forms of entertainment developed, and technology became an important part of gaming. When personal computers became common in the 1990s, and tablets and smartphones became widely available and preferred in the twenty-first century, the fields of gaming and entertainment overlapped even more.

A SLIGHTLY LESS BRIEF HISTORY OF ENTERTAINMENT AND GAMING

While gaming has always been a *form* of entertainment (people play games for their entertainment, after all), the two fields began separately but eventually grew to cross over each other.

ENTERTAINMENT THROUGH THE YEARS

When entertainment consisted of storytelling, dance, books, and even plays, technology was mostly irrelevant. Oral traditions were passed on at gatherings of family and friends, and dance required little more than instruments and space to move. Plays were performed in the daylight, in open-air theaters. If they were performed indoors, candles were used for lighting.

Eventually, technology gave people more flexibility in entertainment. With the advent of electricity and the lightbulb in the 1800s, plays could be performed indoors and at any time of day or night. Dance could be performed to music played on a phonograph or radio. Families could gather around the radio to hear popular radio shows.

Radio eventually gave way to television as the common form of entertainment in family homes. Commercial television broadcasting began in 1947, and by the mid-1950s more than half of all homes in the United States had a television set. The choice of programming was limited, and families generally watched together, but as time went on more channels and programming became available.

Films were popular too. In the early twentieth century, films were "silent," with no audible dialogue. In the late 1920s, beginning with 1927's *The Jazz Singer*, films began to pair spoken words and sound. "Talkies" soon took over the film market, with silent films being a thing of the past.

For a long time, books remained relatively untouched by technology. Printing methods changed and book printing became automated, but for readers as consumers of books, very little changed—books were still printed on paper, bound, and held in one's hands. Eventually, technology changed the publishing industry too. By the 2000s, electronic books were available. They could be read on e-reader devices or on a computer, tablet, or smartphone. While physical books still exist today, more and more people now read books in electronic formats.

GAMING THROUGH THE YEARS

People have played games for centuries. For example, the popular Chinese game mah-jongg was developed in the 1600s. It's thought that the strategy game mancala was played before the seventh century—perhaps even as far back as 1000 BCE. Similarly, chess, checkers, and backgammon were all created more than one thousand years ago. Card and dice games began to grow in popularity in the fifteenth, sixteenth, and seventeenth centuries, before the United States was formed.

When colonists came to America, they brought with them games from other nations, including card games, dice games, and board games like checkers and chess. The dice game craps—a popular casino game now—was inspired by a similar game played in France, and another popular casino game, roulette, was inspired by similar English games.

Eventually, US companies began to develop and distribute new board games, such as Monopoly, which was created by Parker Brothers in 1935 and is still played today. Monopoly now has many forms—some incorporate electronics, but many are still simple board games that look much like the original game.

Board games for children, teens, and adults continued to be popular in the United States throughout the twentieth century, as did card and dice games. Table games like pool were also popular, and Americans continued to enjoy sports as a form of gaming too.

It's little surprise, then, that when technology became a part of gaming, some of the early video games resembled these games people had loved for years.

As shown in this mosaic from the third century CE, dice games have been around for centuries.

WHEN CODING ARRIVED ON THE SCENE

Coding came on the scene for gaming and entertainment around the same time, though both fields remained separate for a while before they began to cross over each other. One of the earliest examples of a video game was presented at the 1939/1940 World's Fair in New York. It was a computer that played a game called nim. Nim had originated in China in the sixteenth century. In it, players remove objects from a pile, and the object of the game can be either to take the last object from the pile or to *not* take the last object from the pile, depending on the version played. In the 1940 computerized version, the object for players was to *not* pick up the last object. The device, called Nimatron, won at least 90 percent of the tens of thousands of games it played against people at the World's Fair.

At that time, computers were *huge* machines, roughly the size of a tall bookcase. They were also extremely expensive, so people didn't have computers in their home to play games. Early video games like Nimatron were mostly for demonstration. In the 1950s, coders experimented with writing chess, checkers, and military strategy games on these large computers, which were often IBM machines. Apple Computer and its associated devices weren't around yet, and gaming consoles were far from being invented.

In the 1950s, the people creating games were usually scientists or mathematicians, since there wasn't a simple, accessible programming language that was easy for nonscientists to learn. But in 1964, two students at Dartmouth College, John Kemeny and Thomas Kurtz, developed the BASIC language. BASIC, an acronym for Beginner's All-purpose Symbolic Instruction Code, was created, like its name suggests, to be an easy programming language that anyone could learn.

Indeed, it was a relatively simple language to understand and master, so the creation of BASIC opened up the field of coding to many more people, resulting in many more

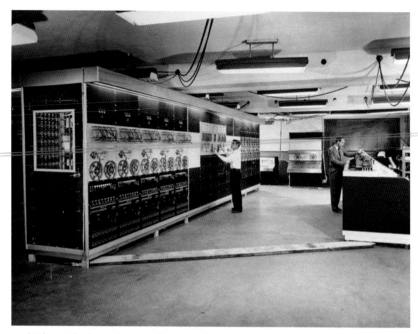

In the early days of computing, mainframe computers were as large as an entire room!

computer games. However, at that time computers still were not in many private homes, so the general public didn't have access to video games.

In 1966, German-born Ralph Baer, who was living and working in the United States, came up with the idea of creating a device that would allow people to play video games on their television sets. The next year, he released the "Brown Box," which allowed users to play games such as tennis on their television sets. The Brown Box was the prototype for the first video game console made for home use, the Magnavox Odyssey, which was released in 1972.

When gaming consoles such as the Odyssey were first released, they weren't terribly common. Many households in America did *not* have consoles, and for a lot of kids the only way to play video games was to go to an arcade or pizza parlor. In 1972, Atari released *Pong*, one of the earliest so-called arcade games. With its simple two-dimensional Ping-Pong simulation, *Pong* was quite popular—in fact, it is widely thought to be the first video game to achieve commercial success. *Pong* was successful enough that, in 1975, Atari released a version for home video game consoles.

At the time of *Pong*, 2D graphics were the only option. Players didn't seem to mind, though. Two dimensions allowed for the creation of landscapes realistic enough for skilled coders to make fun, interactive games, such as *Maze Wars*, which introduced the gaming world to first-person shooter games.

In-home video game consoles became much more popular in 1977, when Atari released their Atari 2600 video game console. Users could play different games by switching cartridges, and a simple joystick with a single red button was all that was needed for most games. The graphics were blocky and two-dimensional, but they were in color, which was a win with home gamers.

One of the best-known early video games is Namco's *Pac-Man*, which appeared for home video game consoles and in arcades in 1980. In 1982, Namco gave a nod to gender equality by releasing the wildly popular *Ms. Pac-Man*, which followed the same basic strategy but featured a character with a bow and lipstick.

Those early Atari machines and arcade games also featured a popular game known as *Donkey Kong*. *Donkey Kong* might be little more than a memory, except that it spawned one of the best-known video game characters to date: Mario. (He was known as Jumpman in *Donkey Kong*, but he went by his given name when he was spun off into the Mario Brothers series of games.)

Video games, coding, and entertainment finally crossed paths in 1982, when Walt Disney Productions released *TRON*, a sci-fi film about a coder who is trapped inside a computer and interacts with its programs. The movie was so popular that it inspired an arcade game.

Shortly thereafter, in 1983, the United States experienced a crash in the video game market. Many people had consoles by that time, and there were a lot of games available. However, personal computers were becoming more popular, and there wasn't really much new in the console world to grab people's interest.

The video game market picked up again when Nintendo released their first console, the Nintendo Entertainment System (NES), in the United States. New games for the

NES hit the market, revitalizing the interest in video game consoles. *The Legend of Zelda* was one such game, and it has been a popular role-playing game ever since.

In 1989, Nintendo released the Game Boy, a popular handheld gaming console. In some ways, the Game Boy was a precursor of today's smartphone games—it was portable, so gamers could play whenever and wherever they wanted.

Software giant Microsoft tapped into another market when they began releasing *Solitaire* for free with their Windows operating systems in 1990. At that time, many professionals, academics, and students used Windows-based personal computers, and even those who didn't own a console could quickly launch *Solitaire* and play a few hands.

Kids in the late 1970s and early 1980s longed to own an Atari 2600 video game console. By today's standards, the system was very primitive!

In the early 1990s, the internet became widely available to the general public, which resulted in a whole new type of play: online gaming. Players could log on to the internet and play against other people. Particularly popular were MMORPGs, or massively multiplayer online role-playing games, which were role-playing games played online in large social communities. *Ultima Online*, released in 1997, is one of the earliest popular MMORPGs.

Companies such as Sega, Sony, and even Microsoft eventually followed Nintendo into the video game console business, but Nintendo took it a step further in 2006, when they managed to combine the activity of sports and the passive entertainment of electronic gaming with the release of the Wii. Wii controllers could sense movement and transmit it to the screen for game play. So a player bowling with the Wii would swing the controller in the same way one would swing one's arm to release a bowling ball, and the player's onscreen character would copy the movement and release the onscreen ball.

The following year, gaming continued its movement toward interactive use when games like *Rock Band* were released. Players could use a special guitar, drums, or microphone to jam along with their favorite bands and compete against other players in a virtual "Battle of the Bands."

VIDEO GAME ADDICTION

The jury is out on whether video game addiction is a real thing. Parents of the past couple of generations have lamented their children spending too much time on video games and getting "addicted" to them, but the psychological community is undecided. The DSM-5, the manual used by psychologists and psychiatrists to diagnose mental disorders, considers video game addiction a "condition of further study," meaning they are undecided on whether it's a diagnosable disorder or not. A 2017 study by Cardiff University in Wales found that out of more than 2,300 adults who regularly played online games, only nine actually met the criteria for an addiction—that's a mere 0.3 percent!

However, video games can certainly be habit-forming, even if not addictive. Regular gamers can get so involved in their gaming world that sometimes they forget to attend to other parts of their lives, such as school or work.

There's an upside for gaming enthusiasts: if they also have the skill and interest to be a coder, there's a world of opportunity for them career-wise. The best careers are ones people feel passionate about, and if a skilled coder is also a passionate gamer, game programming can be a legitimate career path.

At the same time, the internet was continuing to develop. Whereas at first internet access had relied on slow dial-up connections on an active phone line, it wasn't long before high-speed internet through cable and digital subscriber lines became available, and cell phones even had rudimentary games on them.

In the 2000s, smartphones were developed and released by companies such as Apple, LG, and Microsoft. These smartphones had data plans that allowed users to connect to the internet, thus opening up another platform for gaming. Early smartphone games were relatively simple, like *Angry Birds*, but eventually augmented reality entered the scene, used in games such as *Pokémon GO*.

Meanwhile, as the game industry continued to grow and change, the entertainment industry continued to churn out popular television shows and movies. In 1977, George Lucas's *Star Wars: Episode IV* turned the visual-effects industry on its head with the first extensive use of three-dimensional computer animation. The entire film is a special-effects masterpiece, but the scene in which Rebel pilots view the computer-generated model of the Death Star as they prepare to attack it is an important milestone in the history of computer animation in film.

After *Star Wars*, many blockbuster films used 3D animation to create stunning visual effects. Moviegoers were drawn in by films boasting ever more complex visual effects, such as the *Star Trek* films and a great many films by filmmaker Steven Spielberg, who has spent decades making some of the best-known films in history.

Animated films got a reboot when Pixar entered the scene. For years, Disney had produced many of the animated films on the market. In 1995, Pixar released the wildly successful *Toy Story*, the first fully computer-

Pixar's *Toy Story* was wildly popular because it was a good story—but it was also acclaimed for being the first fully computer-animated feature film.

animated feature film. Since then, Pixar has produced more than twenty animated films, most using a programming interface called RenderMan, which allows animators to create movements in 3D animations.

All of this development in both entertainment and gaming would not have been possible without coders. RenderMan software is great, and users don't have to have a coding background to use it. But who created it? Coders. Who created the many other animation and modeling tools on the market for use in games and movies, such as 3ds Max and Maya? Coders. Who created all those many video games played on the Atari, Nintendo, Windows computer, internet, or smartphone? Coders. A video game console is nothing without the games that run on it, and those games were all created by coders.

It's easy to see the incredible impact that coders have had on both the gaming and entertainment industries. Without coders, there wouldn't be an exciting future of new gaming and entertainment technology to look forward to.

CODING AND AUTISM

Diagnoses of autism have been on the rise in the United States for some years. A 2018 study at Johns Hopkins University in Baltimore, Maryland, showed a diagnosis of autism in around 1 of 59 children—roughly 1 in 38 among boys and 1 in 152 among girls. People on the autism spectrum are considered neurodiverse, meaning their brain works a bit differently from that of the general public. That doesn't necessarily mean better or worse, just different.

Companies are beginning to recognize the value that people with autism bring to certain fields, one of which is coding. Often, people with autism are particularly skilled at logical thinking and recognizing patterns—both skills that make good coders. Many people with autism are also particularly strong in visual learning, and coding is a visual task. People with autism also often have a very strong ability to focus on minute, or small and focused, tasks—also a plus in coding.

The tech industry is recognizing that some of the common characteristics of people with autism make for very good coders, and some tech companies, such as Microsoft, SAP, and HP, don't see autism as a disability, but rather as a strength. Given the high unemployment rates overall for people with disabilities, this shift toward hiring people with autism for the unique skills they bring to the table is a positive one.

A virtual reality headset and controllers allow this gamer to climb inside a virtual boxing ring for a match.

chapter_03

Important and New Technologies

One truth about the gaming and entertainment industries is that they are always changing. The effects and graphics used in movies and games even just a decade ago look primitive compared to the spectacular effects and graphics created more recently. This means that for people interested in a career in coding for games or entertainment, the field is always changing, and coders have the opportunity to learn new things all the time.

COMMONLY USED CODING LANGUAGES FOR GAMING

While there are always new technologies being developed and implemented in the gaming and entertainment worlds, a few coding languages have remained relevant and important. The languages are of two types: they may be used for systems programming or web programming. As the name suggests, web programming is used for applications that are run on the web. Systems programming is for stand-alone applications that run on specific devices, such as a video game that runs on a gaming console.

C LANGUAGES

There are a number of C programming languages. The primary one, called simply C, was developed in the early 1970s and is the most often used programming language of all time. One of the strengths of C is that it's a cross-platform language. It can be used to implement programs on different operating systems, including Windows, macOS, and Linux. The C language does not require much run-time support, which makes it a good choice for programming resource-intensive games.

C has spawned a number of related languages, such as C# (called "C sharp") and C++. Currently, C++ is the C language most commonly used in game programming. C++ is object-oriented, meaning the code to run various processes is organized into reusable chunks (called "classes" and "objects," thus the "object-oriented" descriptor). Both C++ and C# are used for systems programming.

Some game engines, such as Unreal, only accept scripts written in C++. The Unreal engine is used as the platform to develop many games, so learning a language that will work on Unreal and is known for being cross-platform is a wise choice. The only downside is that C++ is not the easiest language to learn. However, very few things come without a learning curve, and knowing C++ certainly makes aspiring game coders marketable.

C# is also a somewhat commonly used programming language in the game development world, but it's not used as often as C++. It is, however, used for the Unity 3D game engine.

JAVA

Another commonly used language for systems programming is Java, which was developed in 1995. The strength of Java is that Java scripts can run on any platform that supports Java, without the coder needing to recompile them. (Some cross-platform scripts need to be recompiled for different platforms.) Many, many platforms support Java, so it's a very portable language in that sense—a program written in Java is likely able to run on almost any device.

Java is actually not entirely different from C and C++; some of its syntax was derived from C languages. That's another reason why an aspiring coder would do well to learn C++: not only is it widely used in game programming, but

```
document.getElementById(div)
    else if (i==2)
    {
        var atpos=inputs[i].indexOf('');
        var dotpos=inputs[i].lastIndex
        if (atpos<1 || dotpos<atpos+2
            document.getElementById('errEmail'
        else
            document.getElementById(div).
    }
        if (i==5)
```

Coding languages may look like gibberish at first, but they're actually highly logical languages with conventions just like any spoken language.

it's also the basis for a number of other simpler languages. If a coder knows C++, it is usually not difficult for him or her to learn a language like Java.

JAVASCRIPT

JavaScript sounds like Java, but it's actually quite different. Java is used for systems programming, though Java components can run on the web as well. JavaScript, however, is a web programming language. In fact, it is a critical technology used in the development of the web. According to a 2018 report, nearly 95 percent of all websites use JavaScript. Some of the best-known websites use it, including YouTube, Facebook, Wikipedia, and Amazon.

JavaScript is used to enable interactive web pages and to make things happen on a page. Most web pages have *something* happening on them—users interact with the site in some way. In such cases, JavaScript is nearly always used. In the few cases when a website is completely static, with no interaction, JavaScript may not be needed. But those cases are few and far between, so coders interested in a future career in any sort of web programming would do well to learn JavaScript.

HTML5

Along with JavaScript, a commonly used web programming language is HTML5. HTML, which stands for HyperText Markup Language, was the common language used when the web was first created. It has since evolved and currently exists as HTML5. Web pages are structured and built using HTML5, while JavaScript enables the ability to interact with those pages. HTML5 is quite a powerful language, and sometimes it can be used in place of JavaScript. But in general, any coder interested in a career in some sort of web programming would do well to learn both languages.

CSS3

HTML5 does not work alone in structuring web pages. It is generally used alongside CSS3. CSS stands for Cascading Style Sheets. Style sheets essentially contain all the information about the presentation of a web page—the colors, fonts, and layout.

If a website has, for example, thirty pages contained on that site, a coder would have to specify the fonts, colors, and layouts on each of those thirty pages. Or, to save time, the coder could use CSS3 to specify that the same fonts, colors, layouts, and general presentation should appear on each page of the site.

Imagine a site like Amazon. It has thousands or millions of different pages, depending on a user's search. Specifying the presentation format for each page would be nearly impossible. A style sheet, however, can ensure that each page of results looks more or less the same—uniform—as any other page on Amazon.

CODING FOR ANIMATION AND EFFECTS

For coders interested in a career in animation or visual effects, the languages used are pretty similar. All that's really needed is a language that can display graphics, which includes the C languages, Java, HTML5, CSS3, and JavaScript. One other language that can be useful is Python, which was released in 1991.

Python is a general-purpose programming language that can run on many different operating systems. It is known for being simple and readable, and it supports many

Autodesk's 3ds Max software is a widely used tool in the field of animation and effects.

tasks and components, including databases, graphical user interfaces (GUIs), and multimedia.

Working with animation and visual effects often means using preexisting software, such as Maya or 3ds Max or RenderMan, but there are opportunities for coders interested in careers in the entertainment field, since someone has to create the software packages animators and effects specialists use.

NEW TECHNOLOGIES IN GAMING AND ENTERTAINMENT

Today, there are a number of new technologies in the gaming and entertainment worlds, including facial and voice recognition and virtual and augmented reality.

VIRTUAL AND AUGMENTED REALITY

Recently, gaming and entertainment have been combined in a way that used to exist only in the world of sci-fi: through the use of virtual reality and augmented reality.

Virtual reality (VR) and augmented reality (AR) are two different, but related, technologies. Virtual reality transports the user into a completely virtual world—through a device such as a headset, users become part of the virtual world. Augmented reality, on the other hand, takes the actual world in front of a user and adds elements to it.

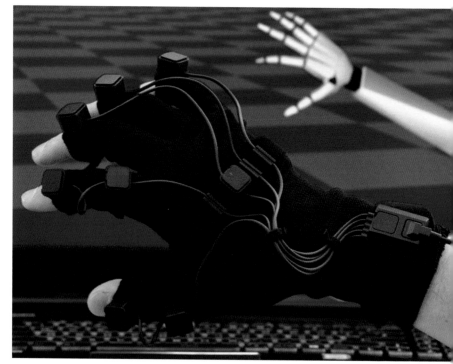

This glove is designed to read and record movement for a virtual reality experience.

An example of large-scale virtual reality is the Toy Story Midway Mania attraction at several of the Disney theme parks. Riders of Midway Mania wear 3D glasses and ride vehicles that go through a number of 3D virtual worlds, playing carnival games along the way. As the riders go through the ride, they play shooting games, throwing games, and a ring-toss game, earning points as they go. It's both game and theme-park ride all in one.

This is all accomplished by a control system that has three components: for the games, for the special effects, and for the ride itself. All three components have software that must work seamlessly for a realistic VR experience. Behind the creation of all that software was a very large team of coders.

Pokémon GO is a great example of augmented reality in action. The game, run on mobile devices, takes the actual environment a person is in and overlays Pokémon creatures onto it. The game runs on the Unity 3D engine, so C# programming would've been a requirement for the game development team.

The Unity 3D engine is used for a lot of VR/AR applications, but the Unreal engine is widely used as well. C++ is supported by Unreal, so in the case of VR/AR development, it would be wise to know the two languages used by the Unity 3D and Unreal game engines: C# and C++.

For any sort of development for VR or AR, many programming languages can work, but the important thing is to find one in which the code is fast—it needs to support a high, consistent frame rate.

Back in the earlier days of gaming and animation, characters and effects sometimes took a while to render— you had to wait for the entire graphic to load and to then animate in the way it was intended. Slow rendering will destroy the "reality" of an AR or VR experience, which is why it's most important to code in a language that will deliver fast performance.

The C languages (C, C#, and C++) are popular for VR and AR programming, and so are Java, JavaScript, and Python.

FACIAL AND VOICE RECOGNITION

Handheld controllers can do a lot, but new technology has allowed people to use voice commands in games, and that technology has expanded beyond gaming too. Devices like the Amazon Echo and Google Home respond with great accuracy to voice commands, allowing users to perform many tasks without so much as picking up their smartphone or laptop.

Facial recognition doesn't let users necessarily control their games—yet. However, new technologies may allow

RealSense

Intel has long made microprocessors, chips, and circuits, but they are also the pioneers behind the RealSense technology. RealSense allows cameras and related devices to "see" and process depth perception. A traditional camera, no matter how powerful, sees and displays the world in two dimensions. Pictures can *look* somewhat three-dimensional depending on the perspective the photographer has used, but they are always two-dimensional—that's what the camera sees and produces.

RealSense cameras and devices, though, use depth and positional tracking to detect depth and see and render the world in three dimensions. The technology has been used for facial recognition and gesture control in gaming, and can also be used for operating drones and robots, among other devices. Programming languages used for the development of applications using RealSense include C, C++, C#, and Python.

Facial recognition software is used for matters of security, but it can also be used in gaming.

games to adjust based on the emotions reflected in a gamer's face. Additionally, facial recognition technology allows people to create avatars to use in gaming, social media, and more.

GESTURE CONTROL

The same basic technology used for facial recognition allows gamers to simply use hand gestures to control their movements in the game world. It's similar to how the Nintendo Wii uses a handheld controller to track and reflect movement, only there's no controller involved—there's a 3D camera that tracks movement.

All of these new technologies and more require coders to create them. They are just a few examples of how technology is always changing, and there's always something new and exciting on which aspiring coders can work.

Those interested in a career in coding for gaming or entertainment have a lot of options within the fields.

chapter_04

Coding Career Options

Not only is it possible to pursue a career in coding for games or entertainment, it's also relatively easy! The work itself isn't easy—coding requires brains, aptitude, and the time and effort to learn programming languages, platforms, graphics, and game engines. However, it's easy in that the industry is wide open—particularly in gaming. Coding in the entertainment field is a bit more of a niche market. There are jobs in that field, but that part of the industry is more specialized. Many of the technical positions in entertainment involve using software that has already been created—not coding. Still, to pursue a job in coding, all that is needed is the background, skills, aptitude, and interest.

WHAT ABOUT A DEGREE?

Coding careers offer many different opportunities. It's always a good idea to get a proper education before diving into the professional world. However, the interesting thing about coding as a career is that you don't always *need* a college degree. A degree is great, and it can certainly open some doors that wouldn't otherwise be open to you, but there *are* jobs for coders who have experience but no formal degree. An aptitude for coding and a background in certain coding languages, such as C++ and C#, can be enough to get a foot in the door for some entry-level coding jobs.

For those who don't just want an entry-level position, a degree is invaluable. Typically, people interested in coding for a living earn a computer science degree. This program of study is widely offered, and many universities have both bachelor's and master's programs in computer science. There are also related degrees specifically in computer programming, software engineering, information technology, computer engineering, and information systems security.

The degree path to follow depends on a person's ultimate job goals. Generally, a degree in computer science is a good starting point for aspiring coders. Computer science programs cover everything from mathematical, scientific, and computational principles to algorithms and software and hardware design.

A college degree isn't necessarily a must to get a job in programming—but it will open many more doors.

A bachelor's degree in computer science helps open more doors to employment in the industry, but to open even more, a master's in computer science or a related field is helpful. Master's programs in computer science usually cover higher-level math and theory, as well as artificial intelligence and computer systems. After completing a master's program in computer science, most people will have learned how to design, code, test, and debug software; design and implement algorithms; and use existing software tools to build entirely new software systems.

To think about how to fashion a future career in coding, it's useful to examine some of the jobs available in the field.

CODING CAREERS IN ENTERTAINMENT

Jobs for coders go by a number of different titles, which are relatively interchangeable. Some job postings call for "coders," others call for "programmers," and still others call for "software engineers" or "software developers." Either way, the jobs are similar, and a coder is typically suited for any of them. They all describe a skilled person who writes code to accomplish certain tasks or to produce a software package or application.

Reviewing the qualifications required for any jobs with these titles or similar ones will reveal whether a person is indeed qualified for a job. For example, a job posting at Pixar for a graphics software engineer included the following in its qualifications listing:

- Highly proficient in C++

- Adept knowledge of modern rendering architectures for rasterization or tracing

- Bachelor's degree in computer science or equivalent

- Experience working in a Linux development environment

- Experience working with 3D applications, such as Maya, Houdini, and Katana

This position was for someone to work on the team to develop Pixar's proprietary animation software. While some of the terms might sound foreign depending on a person's background, someone who has invested time in learning coding and graphics and who has earned a degree in computer science will likely have the background and skills necessary to apply for this position or a similar one.

It's worth noting that Pixar has pretty high qualifications for its incoming coders. Some companies, such as Amazon, don't require a degree and are more interested in hiring skilled coders—whether they have an official college degree or not.

Disney is another major player in the entertainment industry, and it hires coders in many different areas—in its television and movie production studios, but also in its theme parks. A job posting for Disney Parks and Resorts in Southern California required a bachelor's degree in computer science *or* related work experience. The posting did list as "preferred" that applicants have one to three years of experience in coding and developing scalable software components and/or client-facing web applications, but the full diploma was not required.

This particular position called for a coder who could work under minimal supervision. He or she would be coding in a relatively entry-level position, rather than one managing an entire software implementation. Applicants were expected to be able to write code, write tests for it, perform the testing, and debug the code. That is, coders needed to be able to not only write code but also know how to try to break it—and fix it so it's break-proof.

This is called quality assurance (QA). Performing quality assurance is generally expected of those pursuing coding careers. Many companies have specific QA teams to try to "break" the software and identify vulnerabilities in it, but a skilled coder will have tested and worked out most of the bugs before the QA team takes over.

CODING CAREERS IN GAMING

While there are coding careers in entertainment, there are far more in gaming. Gaming is everywhere—on consoles, on computers, on smartphones, on the internet, woven into theme park experiences, and the list goes on. All of these games have coders behind their creation—usually teams of coders, all working on pieces of the application.

Zynga, a prominent game development company, lists many coding opportunities worldwide on its "Careers" web page. For example, a software engineer position for the iOS platform was based in Turkey, and listed among its requirements were the following:

CODING IN A GALAXY FAR, FAR AWAY

In the entertainment industry, Lucasfilm is one of the best-known companies. George Lucas's *Star Wars: Episode IV* was a groundbreaking masterpiece of visual effects, the likes of which had not been seen in the mid-1970s, when the original movie was released.

One of Lucasfilm's memorable characters, Darth Vader

Lucasfilm has continued to break new ground in entertainment in the decades since the release of *Episode IV*, and a coder with a passion for entertainment can land the job of a lifetime working with the team at Lucasfilm.

For example, one segment of Lucasfilm is ILMxLAB. It specializes in real-time immersive entertainment—or virtual reality. ILMxLAB hires programmers for what they call "a crazy-fun, hybridized fusion of entertainment where exceptionally high-end [visual effects] meet interactive, immersive stories." Artists, engineers, and coders work together and delve into artificial intelligence, animation, player controls, and physics to create these VR experiences. It's fast-paced and exciting, and the possibilities for design and effects are limitless—the perfect job for coders who love entertainment and gaming!

- Bachelor's or master's degree in computer science or a related field

- Expert coding skills in Objective-C and comfort learning other programming languages, such as C++ and Swift

- Profound knowledge of game engines, especially Unity

- Strong object-oriented skills, including design, coding, and testing patterns

Good coders need to know how to write the code, but also test and debug it. No doubt Zynga has QA teams, but they expect their coders to do the initial debugging before the code goes to QA.

Zynga is a relatively new company, but one with many career opportunities.

Zynga also requires a degree in computer science or a related field. Once again, that degree will open doors that might otherwise be closed. However, not all game development companies require a degree. Indie game design firms don't always require degrees, and even some of the major players in the field may not, such as Electronic Arts.

Electronic Arts is the company behind EA Sports, a highly successful sports-game development company that produced games such as *Madden NFL*, *FIFA Soccer*, and *Tiger Woods PGA Tour*. A job posting for a software engineer position with EA Sports included the following requirements:

- Bachelor's degree or higher in computer science or computer engineering, or equivalent training and professional experience

- Proficiency in C++ and object-oriented design and implementation

- Experience in both Windows and Linux environments

- Experience with scripting languages (such as Perl, Python, Lua) and C# is an asset

Note that "equivalent training and professional experience" is an option for those who don't have a degree. In other words, an eighteen-year-old with no degree and no professional experience is highly unlikely to get this job, but someone with ten years of related programming experience in a professional setting but no degree might have a chance.

CODING CAREERS IN VIRTUAL AND AUGMENTED REALITY

What about people wanting to code in the latest and greatest marriage between entertainment and gaming: virtual and augmented reality? The requirements are fairly similar to those of other coding positions. For example, a posting for a virtual reality software engineer at tech giant

Many think VR and AR are the "next big thing," and currently careers in them are plentiful.

Google called for applicants to have the following minimum qualifications:

- Bachelor's degree in computer science or related field, or equivalent practical experience
- Sofware development experience in at least one general-purpose programming language
- Experience with VR, including but not limited to 3D graphics, rendering, video and audio codecs, and/or media players
- Experience with mobile development in iOS, Android, and other mobile environments

Pretty basic requirements, right? Notice the word "minimum" before "qualifications." That means more education and experience will be preferred in applicants for this position. Further down the listing, it says that a master's degree or PhD in computer science with an emphasis on graphics is preferred, along with experience in Unity and Unreal game engines and experience designing APIs (application programming interfaces) and SDKs (software development kits).

However, skilled coders without these preferred qualifications shouldn't necessarily be discouraged. There is enough demand for good coders that many companies are willing to overlook a few missing qualifications if an applicant seems like a good candidate for a job.

Tech giant Apple, for example, posted a job listing for an augmented reality experiences programmer, and it listed the following as preferred qualifications:

- **More than five years' experience in game development**

- **Experience working with Swift, Objective-C, and iOS**

- **Experience or prior experience with AR/VR**

- **Bachelor's or master's degree in computer science or equivalent work experience**

However, the job listing also specifically stated, "Motivated applicants are encouraged to apply even if you are missing some of the qualifications." Applying for a position takes nothing more than a little bit of time and effort, so it doesn't hurt for applicants to apply for a position like this, even if they might be missing a qualification or two.

MORE DOORS CAN BE OPENED

In short, for those interested in a coding career in gaming or entertainment, there are opportunities even for those without a degree. However, earning a bachelor's or master's degree in computer science or a related field will open far more doors. The time spent in school is also a good chance to learn new languages and technologies, as well as to network with others in the field—sometimes networking is what opens a particular door to an excellent career opportunity.

If college is not in a student's future for any reason, the field of coding is not closed. Learning marketable programming languages and gaining experience through internships or independent opportunities can result in a promising future career in coding.

Students interested in a career in coding for gaming or entertainment can take steps to prepare themselves while still in high school or even middle school.

chapter_05

Working Toward the Future

For those interested in a career in coding for gaming or entertainment, there's not one single path to follow. There are several roads aspiring coders can take to eventually land a job at the employer of their choice.

THE COLLEGE ROAD

For aspiring coders who want the most doors opened for them, college is generally the best road to follow. Having a bachelor's or a master's degree in computer science or a related field, such as software engineering, will never *close* any doors—a person with a college degree will not be considered overqualified for a coding position.

Computer science and software engineering programs are offered at many colleges and universities, and listing them all would fill an entire (large) book. However, there are certain schools that are known for having particularly strong programs in video game design and development. GameDesigning.org has ranked the top seventy-five programs by considering a number of criteria, including the following:

- **Strong graduation rates**

- **Accredited degree programs**

Academic materials are increasingly moving to online formats, but there are still many books written on how to learn particular programming languages or technologies.

- Average starting salary for graduates

- Transferrable credits to other colleges and programs

- Professor reviews

- Reputation and student feedback

Accreditation is important. Accredited schools have met the minimum standards for higher learning set by a peer review board—meaning accredited schools are generally guaranteed to provide at the very least an adequate education. If a school is not accredited, it may not meet the minimum standard of quality for an institution of higher education. In other words, it might not offer a quality education—and thus a degree from an unaccredited school may not be worth much in the working world. For aspiring coders wanting to pursue a degree, it is highly advisable to *only* consider accredited programs.

Some of the universities GameDesigning.org ranks among the best are the University of Southern California (USC), which has strong ties to the entertainment industry; University of Utah, which has a strong internship program with software developer EA Sports; DigiPen Institute of Technology, which is supported by Nintendo and located near the Microsoft headquarters; and Drexel University and

Carnegie Mellon University, both located in Pennsylvania and both well known for their strong technology programs.

One of the strongest schools for computer science in the United States is Massachusetts Institute of Technology (MIT). Interestingly, MIT does not offer a degree in game development. However, they do have the MIT Game Lab, where students can create their own curriculum of study to focus their degree on game programming.

THE BOOTCAMP ROAD

Another option is to go to what some people refer to as coding bootcamp, an intensive multiweek program in which students learn coding at a rapidly accelerated pace. Bootcamps are often three to four months long (as opposed to the four or more years a bachelor's program involves), so students learn a lot in a very short time.

Flatiron School, headquartered in New York City, is one such bootcamp. They have campuses in New York City, London, Seattle, Houston, and Washington, DC, among other cities. They also have online courses. Flatiron offers courses in Java, Ruby, front-end web development, and general coding. They boast a placement rate for graduates of more than 90 percent—in salaried jobs, paid apprenticeships, and part-time jobs. They are also dedicated to trying to increase diversity in the coding world, which historically has been male-dominated and lacking in black or Latinx coders.

Bootcamps are a great option for students who want to get into the industry quickly or may not be able to attend a four-year college or university for one reason or another. However, coming out of bootcamp, coders usually find they can be hired at the level of junior developer. It's not a bad start, but it's a step down from where coders with a bachelor's degree are likely to be hired.

Flatiron isn't the only coding bootcamp out there—in fact, they are pretty common. SwitchUp.org, a website that helps students find the best bootcamp to help prepare them to enter the technology field, ran a survey of the best coding bootcamps in 2018 and ranked the top fifty. Finding them is as easy as doing an internet search for "best coding bootcamps," but SwitchUp suggests a few important factors interested students should consider:

- **Does the bootcamp offer online courses?**

- **Does the bootcamp offer flexible class schedules for working students?**

- **Does the bootcamp publish an outcomes report that is verified by a third party (in other words, provable data about how their students fare in the job market post-bootcamp)?**

- **Does the bootcamp guarantee job placement after completion?**

INTERNSHIPS

Whichever educational route an aspiring coder chooses, an internship can be a great way to get a foot in the door and learn more about a job and the company at which it's offered. The requirements for internships are much less rigorous than those for permanent employment. Disney Interactive, for example, offers internships for back-end game programmers, and the only firm requirement is that participants must be enrolled in at least one class at an accredited college or university *or* be a recent graduate

An internship allows a student to learn from an experienced mentor in their field of choice and can be a great way to gain experience.

(within the last six months). The requirements for an internship at Sony Interactive Entertainment are a little more demanding. Applicants must have at least two years of coursework toward a bachelor's degree in computer science and must have experience in C and C++. Funkitron, a Massachusetts-based game developer, offers remote internships for students who want to work from home. Their only requirement is that prospective interns be in college or have a college degree, and if they have game design or programming experience, it's a plus.

For coders interested in working in entertainment, Lucasfilm offers paid, twelve-week internships in a number of different positions. Pixar offers paid twelve-week and six-month internships in several different departments, including software research and development, and RenderMan. They also offer paid, one-year residencies in software research and development for recent college graduates. The residencies come with relocation assistance for interested candidates who live outside of the San Francisco Bay Area, where Pixar is headquartered. Disney Animation offers paid twelve-week technology internships for technology students in software or systems engineering, and they have more general internships and apprenticeships for those interested in animation but not necessarily in coding for animation.

CODING ON THE CUTTING EDGE

Pokémon GO is probably the best-known mass-market application of augmented reality thus far.

One of the latest technologies in gaming and entertainment is AR/VR, and there are a multitude of jobs for skilled coders in these fields. One particular company, Lightform, based in San Francisco, is leading the industry by building the first computer made for projected augmented reality—providing users with an AR experience without a headset. Their "creative coder/creative technologist" position is open to coders skilled in C and C++ and who have experience with game engines and shaders. Shaders were originally just what they sound like—programs that help in shading graphics. Now, they do many more graphics tasks beyond simply shading, including visual effects, rendering, and post-processing.

Lightform is a startup company, as are many cutting-edge technology firms. Startups can be risky, though. If they don't succeed, employees are out of a job. However, the rewards can be great, particularly if the startup offers stock options and their product becomes widely used. In addition, tech startups sometimes have fun employee perks. Lightform boasts that their employees get unlimited vacation, access to a cereal bar and lattes, a dog-friendly office, and the opportunity to play with "all the coolest AR/VR gadgets."

THE SELF-TAUGHT ROAD

Back in the early days of programming and development, many programmers were self-taught. This is still a valid way of learning, especially for students who want to increase their knowledge before enrolling in a degree program or bootcamp.

Bookstores have shelves full of books on programming in different languages and for different industries. Learning a programming language can be as simple as picking up a book and sitting down at the computer to work through it. There are even books designed for children who want to learn programming—and plenty available for teens and young adults.

Anyone who wants to learn coding can start by going into a bookstore and browsing the shelves for books on coding and technology.

The internet also has a wealth of knowledge for aspiring coders. Many websites, such as Code.org, allow students to learn coding at their own pace and then practice by creating projects. For students who want to start at the very bottom level, there are websites that teach coding to kids just starting to learn computing. Whatever level an aspiring coder is at, there's an online organization offering free lessons, tutorials, and projects. What's stopping you? Get coding!

Glossary

API An acronym for application programming interface, the tools and resources that allow developers to create software applications.

arcade game A gaming machine installed in a public place, such as a restaurant or a video game arcade.

augmented reality (AR) Technology that places computer-generated images on the user's real-world view.

cross-platform Able to be used on different software platforms.

first-person shooter A game in which the object is to shoot enemies or targets, and the player views the world through the eyes of the character they control.

frame rate The frequency at which frames in a video sequence are displayed.

game engine The basic software on which a video game runs.

interactive A part of a website where users can enter information or perform other tasks.

iOS The name of the operating system used for Apple mobile devices.

microprocessor An integrated circuit that holds the computer's central processing unit functions.

neurodiverse Having brain function and/or behavioral traits outside the norm for the human population.

niche A specialized market segment for a product or service.

object-oriented A form of programming that centers on objects that contain data.

phonograph A record player.

quality assurance (QA) A set of processes designed to test a product.

role-playing game A game in which players control an imaginary character in an imaginary world who goes on adventures or engages in quests.

scalable Able to be used in a range of environments.

SDK An acronym for software development kit, a set of development tools that allow coders to create applications for particular software packages.

shader A computer program used for shading and graphic special effects.

static element A part of a website that does not change.

syntax The arrangement of programming language and commands in an expected form that will enable a computer to produce expected results.

systems programming Coding for stand-alone devices and applications, such as gaming consoles or software packages that are not web-based.

virtual reality Technology that places a user entirely in a computer-generated, simulated environment.

web programming Coding for programs and applications designed to run on a web browser.

Further Information

BOOKS

Conrod, Philip, and Lou Tylee. *Programming Games with Java: A JFC Swing Tutorial.* Maple Valley, WA: Kidware Software, LLC, 2017.

——. *Programming Games with Visual C#: An Intermediate Step by Step Tutorial.* Maple Valley, WA: Kidware Software, LLC, 2017.

Gonzales, Andrea, and Sophie Houser. *Girl Code: Gaming, Going Viral, and Getting It Done.* New York: Harper Collins, 2018.

Rauf, Don. *Getting Paid to Work in 3D.* New York: Rosen Young Adult, 2017.

Vaidyanathan, Sheena. *Creative Coding in Python: 30+ Programming in Art, Games, and More.* Bloomington, IN: Quarry Books, 2018.

WEBSITES

APPINVENTOR
http://www.appinventor.org
For students interested in learning how to create apps, this website offers lessons and tools.

MADE WITH CODE
https://www.madewithcode.com
This site, created by Google, focuses on coding projects that inspire tween and teen girls to explore their interest in coding.

MICROSOFT MAKECODE

https://www.microsoft.com/en-us/makecode?rtc=1

The MakeCode website offers programming projects for aspiring coders at all different levels.

MUSEUMS AND ORGANIZATIONS

BLACK GIRLS CODE

http://www.blackgirlscode.com

This organization helps empower girls of color to learn coding, in an effort to improve the number of women of color in the technology industry.

CODE.ORG

https://code.org

A nonprofit dedicated to helping students learn coding. It offers online courses, labs, and projects for aspiring coders.

DIGITAL MEDIA ACADEMY

https://www.digitalmediaacademy.org

A spinoff from Stanford University, Digital Media Academy offers online courses and STEM summer camps across the United States for kids and teens.

Selected Bibliography

"Animation Programmers and Engineers Creative and Passionate."
Software Engineer Insider. Accessed November 15, 2018.
https://www.softwareengineerinsider.com/careers/animation-
programmer-engineer.html.

Bhargava, Ruchi. "What Is the Best Programming Language for
Games?" Freelancer, July 27, 2017. https://www.freelancer.
com/community/articles/what-is-the-best-programming-
language-for-games.

"11 Unbelievable Advances in Gaming Technology." Mental
Floss. Accessed November 15, 2018. http://mentalfloss.
com/article/61764/11-unbelievable-advances-gaming-
technology.

Flombaum, Avi. "The Multiple Career Paths That Attending a
Coding Bootcamp Can Open Up for You." *Huffington Post*,
October 30, 2017. https://www.huffingtonpost.com/entry/
the-multiple-career-paths-that-attending-a-coding-bootcamp-
us-59f77e33e4b0e4c2eab1c2e8.

"45 Percent of Gamers Are Women. But in Every Other Way,
They're Still Not Equal to Men." Athena40. Accessed
November 15, 2018. https://www.athena40.org/45-percent-
of-gamers-are-women.

"Greatest Visual and Special Effects (F/X)–Milestones in Film
1975–1979." AMC Filmsite. Accessed November 15, 2018.
http://www.filmsite.org/visualeffects10.html.

Intel RealSense (website). Intel.com. Accessed November 15,
2018. https://realsense.intel.com.

Johns Hopkins University Bloomberg School of Public Health.
"U.S. Autism Rate up 15 Percent Over Two-Year Period:
Researchers Say Racial and Ethnic Disparities Are Narrowing."
ScienceDaily. April 26, 2018. http://www.sciencedaily.com/
releases/2018/04/180426141604.htm.

Rayome, Alison DeNisco. "The 7 Most Popular Programming
Languages for AR and VR Developers." TechRepublic.
June 22, 2018. https://www.techrepublic.com/article/
the-7-most-popular-programming-languages-for-ar-and-vr-
developers.

"The 6 Most Important Programming Languages for Game
Design." GameDesigning.org. May 12, 2018. https://www.
gamedesigning.org/career/programming-languages.

Stephens, Mitchell. "History of Television." *Grolier Encyclopedia*.
Accessed November 15, 2018. https://www.nyu.edu/
classes/stephens/History%20of%20Television%20page.htm.

"This Month in Physics History. October 1958: Physicist Invents
First Video Game." *APS News* 17, no. 9 (October 2008).
https://www.aps.org/publications/apsnews/200810/
physicshistory.cfm.

"2019 Best Coding Bootcamps." SwitchUp. Accessed
    November 15, 2018. https://www.switchup.org/rankings/
    best-coding-bootcamps.

"Usage of JavaScript for Websites." W3Techs. Accessed
    October 25, 2018. https://w3techs.com/technologies/details/
    cp-javascript/all/all.

"Video Game History Timeline." The Strong National Museum
    of Play. Accessed November 15, 2018. http://www.
    museumofplay.org/about/icheg/video-game-history/timeline.

Weinstein, Netta, Andrew Przybylski, and Kou Murayama. "A
    Prospective Study of the Motivational and Health Dynamics
    of Internet Gaming Disorder." PeerJ, September 29, 2017.
    https://doi.org/10.7717/peerj.3838.

Weststar, Johanna, and Marie-Josée Legault. Developer
    Satisfaction Survey 2016 Summary Report. International Game
    Developers Association. November 4, 2016. https://cdn.
    ymaws.com/www.igda.org/resource/resmgr/files-2016-
    dss/IGDA-DSS-2016-Summary-Report.pdf.

INDEX

ABOUT THE AUTHOR

Cathleen Small is the author of dozens of nonfiction books for students. Small grew up in the Silicon Valley as the daughter and sister of programmers. She worked as a technical editor for books on coding, software implementations, and IT security for more than a decade. When she's not writing, Small enjoys spending time with her family in the San Francisco Bay Area.